The Slow Build

A Step-by-Step Guide to Financial Freedom

Andrew Galowey

Copyright © [Andrew Galowey] [2024]. All rights reserved. No part of this publication may be reproduced, distributed, or transmitted in any form or by any means, including photocopying, recording, or other electronic or mechanical methods, without the prior written permission of the publisher, except in the case of brief quotations embodied in critical reviews and certain other noncommercial uses permitted by copyright law.

Table Of Contents

Introduction

Chapter 1: Laying the Foundation: Building Your Financial Compass

Chapter 2: Mapping Your Course and Understanding Your Financial Landscape

Chapter 3: Clearing the Path and Conquering Debt

Chapter 4: Building Your Fortress: Saving Strategies for All Goals

Chapter 5: Planting the Seeds: Investing in Long-Term Growth

Conclusion

Introduction

Have you ever imagined a life free of financial worries? Imagine waking up every morning knowing that your expenses have been paid, your future is safe, and you have the flexibility to follow your hobbies. Financial independence is not a faraway ideal; it is a goal that can be achieved via a series of attainable actions. This book, "The Slow Build: A Step-by-Step Guide to Financial Freedom," can help you achieve your ambition.

Here, we'll break down the path to financial freedom into simple, practical steps. We'll go over everything from budgeting and saving to debt management and setting up a solid investing foundation. Whether you're just beginning out on your financial journey or wanting to improve your plan, this book will provide you with the information and skills you need to create a safe and rewarding future. Are you ready to take charge of your money and begin your journey to financial freedom? Let us begin!

Chapter 1: Laying the Foundation: Building Your Financial Compass

Financial independence. It's an often used word that conjures up visions of early retirement, exotic holidays, and a life free of financial burden. However, for many, it seems like a faraway fantasy rather than a practical reality. The fact is that financial independence is not a privilege reserved for a select few. Anyone who is prepared to take charge of their money and lay a firm foundation may achieve this level.

This chapter is the first step on that trip. Here, we'll define financial independence and discuss its importance in living a satisfying life. We'll also discuss the necessity of cultivating a healthy money attitude and conquering any limiting ideas that may be holding you back.

What is financial freedom?

Financial independence does not have a universal definition. It is a personal situation in which you have enough money or fortune to meet your living expenditures without depending entirely on a regular employment. It's about having the freedom to follow your hobbies, whether that's creating your own company, exploring the globe, or just spending more time with loved ones. Financial independence does not imply enjoying an extravagant lifestyle; rather, it entails having options and feeling comfortable about your financial future.

Why is financial freedom important?

Financial independence provides several advantages that go well beyond just having more money in the bank. Here's why it's worth pursuing:

- Reduced Stress: Financial issues are a major cause of stress in our lives. Financial independence offers a safety

net, relieving the pressure of living paycheck to paycheck or worrying about unforeseen bills.
- Increased Control: When you are financially free, you have the freedom to make decisions based on your beliefs and priorities rather than your financial situation. You may choose to work fewer hours, pursue a passion project, or care for your family without fear of financial consequences.
- Greater Security: Life throws curveballs. Financial independence protects against unforeseen circumstances such as sickness, job loss, and economic downturns. It enables you to withstand these storms with little financial difficulty.
- Enhanced Well-Being: Financial independence promotes peace of mind and enables you to concentrate on what really matters in life. It frees up mental space to follow your

interests, strengthen connections, and give back to your community.

Developing a Healthy Money Mindset

Our upbringing, societal influences, and personal experiences all have an impact on how we see money. To obtain financial independence, you must first adopt a healthy money attitude. Here are some important aspects to consider:

- Abundance vs. Scarcity: Change your thinking from scarcity (fearing there isn't enough) to abundance (feeling there is enough for everyone, including yourself). This enables you to concentrate on building money rather than just conserving what you have.
- Gratitude Over Entitlement: Be grateful for what you already have. This promotes a healthy connection

with money and allows you to avoid excessive spending.
- Delayed gratification: Learn to prioritize long-term objectives above immediate cravings. Developing the discipline to save now permits you to have a more fulfilled life tomorrow.
- Financial Knowledge: Arm yourself with information on personal finance. Learn about budgeting tactics, debt management, and investment opportunities. The more you know, the more confident you will be in making wise financial choices.

Overcoming Limiting Beliefs

Many individuals have restrictive views about money that might impede their journey toward financial independence. These may include:

- "I'm not good with money."
- "Rich people are lucky, not deserving."

- "Making a lot of money requires sacrificing everything I enjoy."

Challenge these limiting ideas. Replace them with powerful concepts like "I can learn to manage my finances effectively," "Financial success is achievable with hard work and planning," and "Financial freedom allows me to pursue the things I value most in life."

Financial independence is a journey rather than a destination. This chapter has built the framework by explaining its significance and promoting a healthy financial outlook. Remember, you have the ability to create a greater financial future. In the following chapters, we'll go over the practical actions you may take to attain financial independence, from budgeting and debt management to establishing a solid investing foundation. It's time to take charge, establish your financial compass, and begin your path to a life of liberty and stability.

Chapter 2: Mapping Your Course and Understanding Your Financial Landscape

Congratulations! Establishing a healthy money mentality is the first critical step toward financial independence. It's time to have a better knowledge of your present financial status. Consider this chapter to be the equivalent of grabbing a map and compass; we'll define your starting position and provide you with the tools you need to navigate your financial trip.

Tracking Income and Expenses

Understanding where your money goes is a key component of financial planning. Here's how to efficiently monitor your earnings and expenses:

- Gather Information: Make a list of all your revenue sources, including salaries, side hustles, investment income, and rental income (if appropriate). Gather your bank

statements, credit card bills, and receipts from the last several months.
- Choose Your Tracking Method: There are numerous methods for tracking income and spending. You may use a basic pen-and-paper technique, a downloaded spreadsheet template, or budgeting applications that are easily accessible on your phone or PC. Experiment to discover the system that works best for you.
- Categorize Your spending: Group your spending into categories such as housing, utilities, food, transportation, entertainment, debt payments, and so on. This allows you to see where your money is going and find areas for possible savings.
- Be Honest and Consistent: Tracking may tell a lot about your spending patterns, so be honest with yourself. Commit to constantly tracking your income and spending in order to keep

a clear picture of your financial condition.

Understand Your Cash Flow

After a month or two of tracking your income and spending, it's time to assess your cash flow. This is the difference between the money coming in (income) and going out (expenses). How to Analyze Your Cash Flow:

To calculate your net income, subtract your entire monthly costs from your total monthly revenue. This calculates your net income, which is the amount of money left over after deducting your costs.
- Identify Spending Patterns: Examine your category costs to see where you may be overspending. Are you eating out more than expected? Are subscriptions depleting your funds? Understanding your spending habits enables you to make more educated

choices about how to improve your budget.

Positive or negative cash flow? A positive cash flow indicates that your revenue exceeds your costs, enabling you to save and invest for the future. A negative cash flow means that you are spending more than you make. This means changing your spending patterns or finding methods to boost your income.

Creating a realistic budget.

Now that you've determined your income and spending, it's time to develop a budget, which will serve as a road map for your financial future. Here are some budgeting strategies to consider:

- The 50/30/20 guideline: This popular guideline states that you should spend 50% of your income on necessities (housing, electricity, and food), 30% on desires (entertainment, eating out),

and 20% on savings and debt reduction. You may change these percentages depending on your specific needs.
- Zero-Based Budgeting: This system allocates each dollar of revenue to a specified category, guaranteeing that you do not spend more than you make. It involves more prior preparation, but it may significantly increase your savings.

Budget Tools and Resources

There are several budgeting tools and resources available to help you develop and stick to a budget. Here are a few choices:

- Budgeting applications: Many user-friendly applications let you to monitor income and expenditures, classify spending, and create savings goals all inside the app.

- Online Budgeting Templates: Both free and paid online templates include pre-formatted spreadsheets to help with cost monitoring and budget formulation.
- Financial Advisors: While not necessary for everyone, a financial adviser may provide tailored advice on budgeting and financial planning.

Tracking your income and spending, analyzing your cash flow, and developing a realistic budget are all critical stages toward reaching financial independence. By taking charge of your money and making educated choices based on your present position, you may lay the groundwork for a secure financial future. The next chapters will go over debt management tactics, savings tips, and investment possibilities to help you get closer to financial independence.

Chapter 3: Clearing the Path and Conquering Debt

Debt might seem like a burden that prevents you from achieving your financial objectives. The good news is that with a systematic strategy, you may efficiently manage and reduce debt, freeing up resources for future investments. This chapter provides you with the information and skills you need to overcome your debt and emerge triumphant.

Understanding Different Types of Debt

Not all debt is created equally. Here's a summary of typical debt kinds to help you prioritize your repayment strategy:

- High-Interest Debt: This category includes credit card debt, payday loans, and some retail shop credit. These loans often have high interest rates, which may rapidly add up and considerably raise your total financial load.

Low-interest debt includes mortgages, student loans with low interest rates, and certain vehicle loans. While these debts remain a financial commitment, reduced interest rates make them less urgent to pay off immediately in certain situations.

Debt Repayment Strategies

There are two primary techniques to debt management: the debt avalanche and the debt snowball strategies. Each has advantages, so select the one that best suits your personality and financial position.

- Debt Avalanche: This technique emphasizes repaying debts with the highest interest rates first, regardless of outstanding amount. While it may take longer to pay off each obligation fully, you will eventually save money on interest rates.

- Debt Snowball: This strategy focuses on repaying the lowest debts first, regardless of interest rate. Quick successes like paying off lesser bills may be very motivating and create a feeling of achievement, improving morale and keeping you on track.

Additional Debt Management Tips:

- Negotiate Interest Rates: Contact your creditors and try to get lower interest rates on high-interest bills. Explain your payback plan and see if they are willing to work with you.
- Increase Minimum Payments: Making minimum payments maintains your accounts in good standing, but they do nothing to lower the principle debt. If feasible, attempt to pay more than the minimal amount to speed up your debt payback.

- Review Monthly accounts: Keep an eye out for inaccuracies or fraudulent behavior on your credit card and loan accounts. Catching inconsistencies early might help you save money and avoid future financial troubles.
- Avoid Lifestyle Inflation: As your income rises, fight the temptation to dramatically raise your expenditure. To expedite your efforts, allocate the additional money to debt reduction or savings.

Lifestyle Changes for Debt Reduction

Debt repayment frequently necessitates certain lifestyle changes. Here are some strategies to consider.

- Create a Side Hustle: Look into freelancing options, the gig economy, or starting a small company to supplement your income for debt payback.

- Reduce Discretionary Spending: Examine your finances and eliminate non-essential costs such as eating out, entertainment subscriptions, and impulsive purchases.
- Review Insurance and Utility Bills: Look for cheaper discounts on vehicle insurance, phone plans, and internet service providers. Reducing fixed spending may free up funds for debt payments.
- Sell Unused Belongings: Declutter your home and sell unneeded stuff online or at a garage sale. Use the money to cover extra debt payments.

Live Debt-Free:

While removing debt requires time and effort, the benefits are significant. Debt-free living enables you to save more efficiently, invest more confidently, and face the future with financial certainty. Remember, being debt-free is a marathon, not a sprint. Celebrate milestones along the way, keep inspired, and stick to your debt reduction strategy. As your debt decreases, you will gain momentum and confidence on your journey to financial independence.

This chapter has provided you with the information and skills you need to efficiently manage your debt. The next chapter will go over how to save for emergencies, financial objectives, and, eventually, financial independence.

Chapter 4: Building Your Fortress: Saving Strategies for All Goals

Debt may seem like a never-ending drain, but developing a healthy savings habit is the foundation of financial independence. Savings serve as a safety net, buffering against unforeseen costs and fueling your long-term aspirations. This chapter provides you with excellent ideas for creating a strong savings strategy suited to your specific financial goals.

Importance of Saving

Saving has several advantages that go well beyond financial stability. Here's why prioritizing savings is important:

- Peace of Mind: Having an emergency fund serves as a safety net when confronted with unforeseen costs such as auto repairs, medical bills, or job loss. This relieves financial stress and

helps you to overcome obstacles without incurring debt.
- Saving enables you to follow your ambitions. A solid savings foundation allows you to achieve your objectives, whether they be a dream trip, a down payment on a home, or paying your child's school.
- Savings serve as a platform for future investments. Accumulated savings enable you to invest in stocks, bonds, or mutual funds, which may increase your wealth over time and help you retire.
- Building Financial Discipline: Consistent saving fosters financial discipline. Learning to prioritize long-term objectives above short-term wants is an important skill that improves financial well-being.

Setting SMART Savings Goals

Setting specific objectives is the first step toward successful savings. Use the SMART framework to outline your goals.

- Specific: Determine what you're saving for (emergency fund, down purchase, or retirement).
- Measurable: Determine how much you need to save.
- Attainable: Determine realistic and attainable savings goals based on your income and spending.
- Relevant: Make sure your savings objectives are consistent with your overall financial interests.
- Time-bound: Set a deadline for achieving your savings goal (for example, three months for an emergency fund and five years for a down payment).

Creating an Emergency Fund
An emergency fund is your first line of defense against financial hardship. Ideally,

you should save enough to cover 3-6 months of living expenditures. Here's how to create an emergency fund:

- Automate Savings: Make automatic transfers from your checking account to your savings account. This "out of sight, out of mind" strategy promotes regular savings without requiring effort.
- Start Small: Don't be intimidated by the final aim. Begin with a tiny, reasonable amount that you can easily put away each week or month. Gradually raise the amount as your income permits.
- Use Windfalls: Treat unexpected money, like as tax returns or bonuses, as a chance to increase your emergency reserves.

Saving Strategies for Specific Goals

Aside from the emergency fund, saving for particular objectives requires further forethought. Here are some strategies to consider.

- High-Yield Savings Accounts: Keep your emergency fund and short-term savings objectives in high-yield savings accounts, which provide slightly greater interest rates than regular savings accounts.
- Certificates of Deposit (CDs): CDs are ideal for long-term objectives such as down payments and retirement. These provide guaranteed interest rates but only let you to keep your money for a certain duration.

Take advantage of employer-sponsored retirement plans such as 401(k)s and IRAs. These generally include employer matching contributions and tax breaks to encourage long-term savings.

Maximize Your Savings

Here are some more ways to enhance your savings potential:

- Challenge Yourself: Take part in savings initiatives such as the 52-week challenge, in which you save an increasing amount each week.
- Use Cashback Rewards: Use credit cards with cashback rewards programs and use the earnings to your savings objectives.

Regularly review your savings progress and alter your contributions when your income or expenditures change.

Creating a Habit of Saving

Saving consistently needs discipline and forethought. Here's how to develop a solid savings habit:

- Monitor Your Progress: Stay inspired by tracking your savings progress. Visualize yourself achieving your objectives and celebrating each milestone along the way.
- Reduce Expenses: Identify areas of your budget where you may cut down and redirect those cash to savings.
- Prioritize Saving: Treat saving as an essential cost, similar to rent or utilities. Pay yourself first by automatically putting a part of your earnings to savings before you begin spending.

Creating a solid savings strategy is an important step on your route to financial independence. Setting clear objectives, using proven tactics, and emphasizing continuous saving will help you build a financial fortress to withstand

Chapter 5: Planting the Seeds: Investing in Long-Term Growth

Congratulations! You've developed a healthy money attitude, addressed your debt, and created a strong savings foundation. Now it's time to delve into the realm of investment, the motor that may accelerate your riches toward long-term financial independence. This chapter will teach you the fundamentals of investing, allowing you to comprehend various investment vehicles and establish a smart investment plan.

Understanding the Power of Investment

Investing lets your money work for you. You may possibly increase your wealth over time by diversifying your investments, surpassing inflation and safeguarding your financial future.

Here are some major advantages of investing:

- Long-Term Growth: Stocks, bonds, and other assets have the potential to provide better returns than ordinary savings accounts. This permits your money to compound over time, resulting in dramatically increased long-term financial stability.
- Reaching Financial Goals: Investing may help you reach long-term financial goals such as a comfortable retirement, paying for your child's school, or leaving a financial legacy.
- Hedging Against Inflation: Inflation reduces the buying power of your money over time. Investing in assets that rise with inflation, such as equities, helps to safeguard and preserve your wealth's value.

Types of investment vehicles

The financial environment provides a diverse range of possibilities, each with its own risk-reward profile. Here's a breakdown of several popular investment vehicles:

- Stocks: When you purchase a stock, you are effectively acquiring a tiny share in a firm. Stocks have the potential for big gains, but they also carry the greatest amount of risk. Stock prices may change dramatically according to corporate performance, market circumstances, and macroeconomic reasons.
- Bonds are simply loans given to governments or enterprises. In exchange for your investment, you will receive monthly interest payments and the repayment of your principle amount on the bond's maturity date. Bonds are often regarded less risky than stocks, although they have lesser potential rewards.
- Mutual funds combine money from various participants and invest it in a diverse portfolio of stocks, bonds, and

other assets. Diversification reduces risk and allows novices to invest in a wide range of assets.
- Exchange-Traded Funds (ETFs): Like mutual funds, ETFs are aggregates of assets that trade on stock exchanges alongside individual equities. They provide diversity and cheaper costs than some actively managed mutual funds.

Understanding Risk Tolerance

Investing involves inherent risk. Understanding your risk tolerance, or degree of comfort with probable losses, is essential for effective investment. Here are some things to consider:

- Investment Time Horizon: The amount of time you want to retain your assets is critical. Longer time horizons enable you to ride out market changes and get the benefits of compounding

interest. Investors with shorter time horizons may need to select lower-risk alternatives.
- Financial Goals: Your investing objectives determine your risk tolerance. Aggressive financial objectives may need a higher-risk investing plan, other goals such as accumulating an emergency fund may favor lower-risk choices with assured returns.
- Age: Younger investors often have a longer time horizon and are willing to take on more risk in exchange for possibly bigger profits. As you approach retirement, it's frequently a good idea to transition to a more conservative investing plan to safeguard your acquired money.

Developing an Investment Strategy

Here's how to create an effective investing strategy:

Asset Allocation entails separating your investing portfolio into several asset classes such as equities, bonds, and cash equivalents. The optimal asset allocation depends on your risk tolerance and time horizon. Younger investors with a longer time horizon may allocate a larger proportion to equities for growth potential, but those approaching retirement may choose bonds for stability.
- Diversification: Avoid putting all your eggs in one basket. Diversify your assets among asset classes, sectors, and enterprises to reduce risk. This manner, losses in one area may be countered by improvements in another.
- Rebalancing: To preserve your preferred asset allocation, examine your portfolio on a regular basis and rebalance it as needed. Market movements might cause your asset percentages to shift over time, so

rebalancing keeps your portfolio in line with your risk tolerance and investing objectives.

Getting Started with Investment

There are a few methods to start your investing journey:

Open an Individual Retirement Account (IRA) or Employer-Sponsored Plan: These accounts provide tax breaks to encourage retirement savings.
- Invest with a robo-advisor: Robo-advisors are automated investing systems that generate and manage tailored portfolios depending on your risk tolerance and objectives.

Consult a knowledgeable financial adviser to establish a complete investment plan.

Conclusion

By reaching this moment, you've begun a transforming path toward financial independence. You've formed a healthy money attitude, dealt with debt, established a solid savings foundation, and dabbled in the world of investment. Remember that financial independence is an ongoing process of making educated choices, managing your money properly, and adjusting to changing circumstances.

This book has provided you with the information and resources you need to succeed in your financial path. Don't be afraid to experiment, learn from your mistakes, and adapt your strategy as required. With determination, discipline, and the tactics discussed in these pages, you may achieve financial stability and live a life of freedom and opportunity. The future is yours to create, and financial independence allows for a more rewarding and empowered path. So, take charge, invest in yourself, and watch your financial future grow!

www.ingramcontent.com/pod-product-compliance
Lightning Source LLC
Chambersburg PA
CBHW071221240526
45470CB00018B/2190